BOUNCE

Help Your Child Build Resilience and Thrive in School, Sports and Life

Kate K. Lund, Psy.D.

BOUNCE: Help Your Child Build Resilience and Thrive in School, Sports and Life

Copyright 2017 by **KATE K. LUND, Psy.D.**, Kate Lund Psychology, PLLC.

All rights reserved. No part of this book may be used or reproduced in any manner whatsoever without written permission from **KATE K. LUND, Psy.D.**, except as provided by the United States of America copyright law or in the case of brief quotations embodied in articles and reviews.

The scanning, uploading and distribution of this book via the Internet or via any other means without the permission of the publisher is illegal and punishable by law.

Please purchase only authorized electronic editions and do not participate in or encourage electronic piracy of copyrighted materials. Your support of the author's rights is sincerely appreciated.

Legal Disclaimer:

The purpose of this book is to educate the reader and encourage broad thinking about the idea of building resilience in children. This book is not intended to be a substitute for the advice of a licensed mental health practitioner or certified professional coach. You should seek professional advice about your specific situation.

HeartMath is a registered trademark of Quantum Intech, Inc.

Printed in the United States of America.

ISBN: 978-1-946978-07-3

First Printing: 2017

Dedication

To my father and mother, who fostered resilience by example.

Table of Contents

Acknowledgments vii

INTRODUCTION: How My Story Inspired This Book 1

CHAPTER 1. The Relationship between Resilience and Potential 7

CHAPTER 2. Beyond Resilience: What Else Drives Potential? 13

CHAPTER 3. Tolerating Frustration and Managing Emotions: Pillar One 19

CHAPTER 4. Navigating Friendships and Social Pressures: Pillar Two 27

CHAPTER 5. Sustaining Focus and Attention: Pillar Three 35

CHAPTER 6. Developing Courage: Pillar Four 43

CHAPTER 7. Building Motivation: Pillar Five 53

CHAPTER 8. Finding Confidence: Pillar Six 63

CHAPTER 9. Creating Optimism: Pillar Seven 73

CONCLUSION: What the Kids Have to Say 81

Resource List 91

Author's Biography 93

ACKNOWLEDGMENTS

This book would not have been possible without the guidance, insight and support of many special and important people. First is my father, who provided the initial inspiration for this project by always talking about the book I was going to write. Thanks, Dad. This is that book.

My mother demonstrates resilience every day. Thank you, Mimi, for the example you set.

My husband and boys have been a very important part of this process by offering their unwavering support, which always provides me with energy and direction. Trust me, this project required both in large doses. Thanks, guys.

I also want to thank the students and teachers who contributed ideas and insights so readily to this project – your input has been invaluable.

Thank you to the BSP team, especially Randy Taylor, who went above and beyond in providing insights and guidance during the initial phase of this project. You really helped me to stay on track. Thank you!

Finally, I want to thank my amazing editor, Brenda Newmann, for her incredible guidance, input and technical support throughout the process of pulling this book together. I appreciate what you have done more than you know.

INTRODUCTION

How My Story Inspired This Book

I am a clinical psychologist, a performance coach, a wife, a mother of twin boys, and, once upon a time, I was a child facing significant medical challenges. Because of my personal experience, the question of how children become resilient from an early age has long interested me. In addition to my own experiences, I've had ample opportunity personally and professionally to observe and learn about how children develop resilience and to better understand the connection between resilience and individual potential. That's why my clinical psychology and performance coaching practice focuses on helping people become resilient within their own unique contexts. I've worked with many incredible and courageous people as they have navigated challenges in different domains and come out stronger on the other side.

Some of my most rewarding work has involved helping children and families with medical challenges to develop coping strategies and a new sense of normal in which they can flourish despite the realities they face. As a performance coach, I work with children on navigating challenges and finding ways to be the best they can possibly be, in school and in sports. When children can develop tools to become resilient, they have an essential foundation to navigate the challenges they will inevitably face at school, on the playing fields and beyond. I like to call this foundation their "toolbox" – a set of strategies that they can use to face and overcome challenges. I could have used such a toolbox when I was younger, and that's partly what inspired me to write this book.

My work is influenced by the principles and practices of developmental psychology, positive psychology and emotional intelligence. I also integrate the principles and ideas of HeartMath® and Mental Game Coaching into my work:

- HeartMath is a research-based system of techniques, tools and technology focused on creating balance between our physical, mental and emotional systems. When such balance occurs, we become more resilient and better able to manage stress and challenge. Working with children to learn and integrate the HeartMath skills is particularly powerful and often leads to greater resilience and positive changes across domains, as I have seen time and again in my work with elementary students.

- Mental Game Coaching is a certification program developed by Dr. Patrick Cohn at Peak Performance Sports. The program provides a practical and easily integrated set of tools and techniques for mastering the key skills to build a strong mental game and foundation for sports performance.

The framework for this book is built around many of these principles, ideas and strategies, as I have seen how powerful they are in building resilience and living a resilient life. Within this context, the book presents my vision of the seven pillars of resilience for children during the elementary school years:

1. Tolerating frustration and managing emotions
2. Navigating friendships and social pressures
3. Sustaining focus and attention
4. Developing courage
5. Building motivation
6. Finding confidence
7. Creating optimism

This book is for parents, educators, community leaders and anyone with an active interest in helping children to become resilient and realize their potential. My goal is to present the reasons that resilience is so important for children, while providing strategies for bolstering the resilience of your own child or the children you work with.

Each of the seven pillars of resilience has its own chapter, in which I go into detail and offer composite stories that illustrate real-life situations and challenges children face in school each day, as well as the types of strategies that can help them master these challenges. Each "pillar" chapter ends with lists of action steps. It's important to note that the stories included in the book intentionally combine elements of several different real stories – and use pseudonyms – in order to illustrate an idea or make a point while protecting the identities of the children.

Although I rarely discuss it, I decided to share my own story as a child with medical challenges because it's important to establish a foundation and a context for presenting my ideas on this topic.

My Story

I was a happy and active child, but when I was four years old I started having debilitating headaches and throwing up suddenly, multiple times a day, and often in the middle of the night. At first, my condition baffled the many doctors my parents brought me to. Nobody could figure out why an otherwise healthy and happy four-year-old was having these issues. Finally, a visit to the eye doctor uncovered the problem. He determined that my optic nerves were swollen and I had high pressure in my brain caused by accumulating cerebrospinal fluid. I was diagnosed with hydrocephalus, a condition in which cerebrospinal fluid accumulates in the brain, resulting in a buildup of pressure. The condition is managed with a medical device called a shunt that drains the cerebrospinal fluid when something is preventing it from draining naturally.

Following the discovery of the hydrocephalus, my childhood progressed in a typical manner despite many issues and subsequent surgeries related to problems with my shunt. On numerous occasions, my shunt became blocked and had to be surgically revised. This meant time in the hospital and a period of recovery at home, and a lot of missed school days. Returning to school after each episode was never easy given the fact that part of my head was shaved, and as a result, I had a haircut that was not considered cool.

As we all know, looking different in elementary, middle and even high school is hard in many ways, so this was a challenge, to put it mildly. Yet, I was lucky in that I had great support at home and good friends who didn't let on that they saw anything different about me. I also had a very special dog, Peanut, who was a source of strength and motivation for me from the time I was five years old. I loved that dog with all my heart.

Throughout my childhood and adolescence, I often focused on physical activity as a primary emotional outlet and a way to build strength after each medical setback. And then, in my senior year of high school, my medical story became more complicated. I was captain of the tennis team and was supposed to be at the top of my game, so to speak. Yet, I had not been feeling well or performing well all year, particularly on the tennis court. A series of tests revealed two tumors in my brain, one of which was the underlying reason for my hydrocephalus. In a sense, it was good to know finally why I had the condition in the first place. As a result of this discovery, the next year was extremely challenging both emotionally and physically, with numerous difficult surgeries, the discovery of a third tumor in my spine, and a very long and complicated recovery. College was postponed for a year while I got through this episode – but I did get through it, then went to college and eventually earned a doctorate in clinical psychology.

How I Coped by Focusing on What I *Could* Do

Despite the many challenges my family and I faced throughout my childhood and teenage years, my medical condition was not our defining feature. My parents looked at me as the person I was and did not define me by the condition I happened to have. And they encouraged others to do the same through their own example. This was vital for my sense of self and developing abilities.

So, while I had a vague notion of how these challenges affected me, my parents, family, friends and teachers encouraged me to continue moving forward despite my reality. Their support was instrumental in shaping my resilience. I didn't dwell on how I was different from my friends. The fact is – and this is important – I came to appreciate what I *could* do, as opposed to what I *could not* do, and I went ahead and lived my life.

In school, I realized on some level that I needed to work harder than many of my peers to achieve the same results. At times, this was frustrating, but in the long run working harder was a good thing because it became a habit for me and led me to high levels of academic achievement. I internalized early that positive outcomes required hard work and persistence. And I was fortunate in that the power of hard work, persistence and always doing your best no matter what was reinforced at home every day.

While the obstacles I faced throughout my childhood and adolescence were, quite frankly, miserable both physically and emotionally, they forced me to focus on becoming the best I could possibly be within my own context. This helped me to appreciate and acknowledge individual differences and the fact that we all come to the table from different places and experiences. I learned early to compete with myself, within my own context, and not so much with others. This outlook helped me to live up to my own potential and to maximize my own abilities.

The lessons I learned early have served me well as a psychologist and a mom, and they have been a catalyst for many successes, both personal and professional. While I don't often talk about the parts of my history described in this book, these experiences are embedded into the fabric of who I am. In many ways, they guide my internal compass and inform the way I live my life.

Each one of us has a history. Recognizing and acknowledging our history is part of our journey, and it is an important part of our quest towards building resilience and realizing – and ultimately maximizing – our own unique potential.

CHAPTER 1

The Relationship between Resilience and Potential

Fostering resilience early in students is important because it builds inner strength and makes it possible for children to manage the inevitable challenges and frustrations that arise in school, sports and most areas of their lives. Ultimately, resilience makes it much more likely that children will realize their potential within their own unique context.

WHAT IS RESILIENCE?

Resilience is the ability to bounce back from a setback and move forward. It is the ability to navigate challenges and still succeed.

It's important to foster resilience in children within all their different domains (i.e., home, school, sports) so they can be successful. What does this look like? Here are some examples:

- Better grades
- Improved friendships
- A higher level of overall engagement
- Coping skills for managing challenges
- Belief in self; the courage to try new things in school and sports

The resilient child will be able to answer the questions, "What is possible for me?" and "What do I have to do to get there?"

What Is Potential?

Potential is what we are capable of becoming, or what we are capable of accomplishing as we learn and grow.

Everyone has unique starting points and ending points regarding potential. As we are all individuals, it makes sense that our potential varies in different areas. We have different strengths, interests, passions, opportunities, histories and foundations, and these ultimately have an impact on our potential as human beings. Working with children to help them identify areas of potential early is an important step in helping them to focus on what is possible.

A Developmental Framework

In his landmark work *Childhood and Society,* published in 1950, renowned developmental psychologist Erik Erikson provides a useful context in which to consider human development. He outlines the developmental stages of childhood, with each stage including a central task.

The fourth stage of Erikson's model applies to elementary-school-age children (ages five to twelve) and is called industry (competence) vs. inferiority. The central task of this stage is for children to develop a sense of competence and mastery as they learn and grow. Erikson notes that teachers take on an increasingly important role, along with friendships and peer relationships; the latter often begin to impact a child's sense of self and overall self-esteem.

Children begin to take pride in what they achieve and begin to conceptualize the importance of mastering age-appropriate tasks during this time. Children who receive positive reinforcement and feedback as a result of trying new things and taking initiative develop a sense of competence and confidence in their ability to set and meet goals. Children who don't receive such positive reinforcement, on the other hand, will likely develop feelings of inferiority, which will cause them to doubt their own abilities. The fundamental sense of competence gained through mastering this important stage of development is necessary for children to move in the direction of their potential, Erikson notes. It is the idea that, "I can do this. That might have been hard, but I can do this thing that is so important."

Childhood is a time of developing as human beings – a time of learning and integrating foundational skills and interests. Think about what children learn at school on a social-emotional level: so many important messages about themselves and others, about sharing and trust, about facing and resolving conflict and so much more. The reality is that challenges are part of the school experience, and it is how children can manage such challenges that makes the difference. Within the context of Erikson's model, especially when things are going well, learning to manage challenge is what is important. School is the place where many of these ideas evolve.

The Link between Resilience and Potential

Helping kids, whatever their context, to believe in themselves and what they have to offer is at the core of fostering resilience and maximizing potential. Navigating through and beyond challenges is what allows a child to move in the direction of her potential. Being able to harness inner strength to foster an ongoing sense of possibility, to access and use strengths, and to cultivate a belief in self – despite challenges – creates an inner sense of resilience.

In my own life, I needed to become resilient physically and emotionally as a young child. Early on, my hydrocephalus made certain things more difficult for me than they would have been otherwise. But this provided me with the opportunity to learn how to bounce back after a setback. This was my reality and, over time, it fostered great resilience within me. I learned that it was important to try again when at first I didn't succeed. I learned that hard work and overcompensation allowed me to conquer things that at first seemed impossible. I learned the importance of persistence, facing challenges head-on and trying again when necessary.

It's important to recognize that some children are born more resilient than others. Some have a natural tendency towards resilience, towards bouncing back when something challenging happens. For others, this is a little more difficult. Yet, even for them, resilience can be fostered with proper encouragement and tools.

Resilience is a core element of realizing potential. In thinking about the relationship between resilience and potential, we might consider the following questions: What are a child's strengths? What are his challenges? We then can formulate a plan to capitalize on the child's strengths while helping him to acknowledge and face challenges, overcome fears and work to see challenges as opportunities.

Striving to maximize potential is important because it encourages children to push their limits and to be their very best within their own unique context.

Eric: The Power of Positive Reinforcement

For example, let's consider a little boy named Eric. Eric struggled to read in first grade, and his teachers wondered why, as all other developmental variables seemed intact. His parents worried that he wasn't keeping up, yet they never doubted that their little boy had huge potential despite his early challenges in the classroom.

Eric noticed that he was struggling, but at such an early age he wasn't able to verbalize what he was feeling; his feelings played out mostly through anxiety and some combative behavior at home with his brother and parents.

Educational testing suggested dyslexia, and Eric began receiving help in reading. His reading tutor, along with his mom and dad, noticed Eric's underlying strengths and believed in his potential despite his challenges in the classroom.

Eventually, Eric began to have an easier time in the classroom, his friendships blossomed, and he developed an outgoing and bubbly personality that had been hidden before. He became much less anxious and his attitude about school improved dramatically.

Believing that a child like Eric can succeed despite challenges is vital for many reasons. As Eric started to feel good about himself, positive changes followed in many areas. Important people in his life believed in him, and that made a huge impact on his ability to reach his potential as an early learner. Positive reinforcement can foster resilience by helping children to believe in themselves. Positive reinforcement also contributed greatly to Eric's overall happiness and strengthened his foundation in school and beyond. He learned that he could overcome a challenge, and this set him up for more successes in the future.

CHAPTER 2

Beyond Resilience: What Else Drives Potential?

Chapter 1 looked at how being resilient can help children achieve their potential. This chapter looks at some of the other factors and variables that can also drive potential in children.

EXTERNAL FACTORS

Family, friends and teachers often have an influence in this area. Teachers who encourage, motivate and mentor, and family members and friends who do the same, can be at the core of a child's ability to move towards his potential. My father and mother were great examples of this, as I'll explain below. Believing in a child's potential is a powerful force that instills in the child belief in self and in possibility. When important people in a child's life believe in that child's abilities and possibilities, they foster that child's potential. In turn, they also contribute to resilience by allowing the child to see that it is okay to not succeed on the first try, yet still move forward.

My parents offered me these gifts throughout my childhood, in different ways. My father shared his love of tennis with me from the time I was very young. We were a great team, playing in all the annual parent-child events or just playing together on the weekends. Regardless of the outcome of our matches, we always had fun. On the court, my dad pushed me to become the very best player that I could be, but he never pushed too hard. In this way, he helped me to develop my potential as a tennis player along with a true love of the game. Some of my favorite and most vivid childhood memories involve my dad and me on the tennis court together. Whenever I think of tennis in any context, I always think of my dad and what he meant to me.

My mother also encouraged me to reach my potential. One of my favorite examples of her pushing me beyond my fears to explore possibility was when she encouraged me to start playing golf. I was sitting around one day early in the summer before leaving for college, uncharacteristically melancholy and wondering what to do with myself, when my mother threw me the car keys and said, "Go over to the golf course – you might like it." This was a big deal, since I had not driven alone in a year. (I had been recovering from a prolonged medical challenge related to my hydrocephalus.) Yet, I was ready to take this step and my mother knew it. It was time for me to realize it too, and I am so glad I caught the keys and took that drive to the golf course. It turns out that I love golf and that it's a great fit for me. Thanks to my mom, I became a golfer that summer before college.

Aptitude and Practice

Aptitude is another important variable driving potential. The reality is that students are not inherently good at the same things. They come to the classroom from different places and with different foundations, and educators must honor this reality as they work with students on developing passions and maximizing potential.

For example, pushing children too hard in any area where they don't show a fundamental aptitude or love of what they're doing is unlikely to lead them in the direction of their true potential. It's important to think about that when we hang out with our kids or encourage them to try or do certain things.

Beyond aptitude, the notion of practice and repetition is an important driver of potential. It's rare that someone can jump into something new and do it perfectly. That's why practice is so important, along with the persistence to work hard to improve. In fact, practice alone isn't enough. A Kung Fu instructor I know captured this idea when he said, "Perfect practice makes perfect." We should not just practice, but also practice to the best of our ability.

INTERESTS AND STRENGTHS

The idea of building resilience and maximizing potential through interests, strengths and experiences (both positive and negative) plays out clearly in the classroom. Let's consider Danny, a shy boy who hasn't appeared very engaged in class in first or second grade. He also tends to get easily frustrated when he doesn't understand ideas presented in class. Danny has developed a reputation as a generally unengaged and unapproachable student; as a result, nobody has paid much attention to him. His teachers and classmates don't know him very well. This is a shame, because the reality is that his teachers didn't give him a chance to demonstrate his true capabilities.

It's not until Danny enters third grade that his teacher, Mr. Y, realizes this and makes a concerted effort to get to know and understand Danny. Mr. Y discovers that Danny has a huge imagination and lots of innovative ideas that could foster his learning if given the chance. Mr. Y implements a structured approach for Danny to harness his ideas and get them down on paper as part of his daily literacy unit. As Danny becomes more and more engaged in this process, he also becomes more and more engaged in the general classroom community. As a result, Danny is a happier boy overall and his academic performance improves across the board, along with his social relationships and even his relationships at home. Most importantly, Danny begins to develop an improved sense of himself and a true belief in his own abilities. This belief in self and ability can make all the difference to kids by helping them become resilient learners and realize their potential in the classroom.

The example of Danny shows the power that teachers have when they encourage growth in students by capitalizing on their strengths and abilities.

Facing Challenges

Moving forward in the face of challenges is another important aspect of building resilience. Emily is a young equestrian who has been entering horse shows for a few years. One day, she's out on a trail ride with a group when something spooks the horses and they go out of control. Emily's horse throws her, and she lands hard on the ground amid a stampede of 1,100-pound animals. Clearly, this experience leaves her scared and disillusioned. But Emily's parents acknowledge her fear and their own while encouraging her to think about getting back on the horse. Although it's become a cliché, this idea of getting back on the horse is vital. Giving up would take many opportunities away from Emily, and she wouldn't realize her potential as a rider. In time, Emily overcomes her fear and gets back on the horse; thus, she is in a place to realize her potential as a rider.

At this point, anything in riding seems possible to Emily, and this sense of possibility and belief in herself is becoming evident in many other areas of her life. In this way, the challenge that Emily faced on her horse became an opportunity for her to learn from a scary experience and to move forward in a stronger and better way. No one is immune to challenge, so we can all learn from this important idea: the ability to turn challenge into opportunity can make all the difference. Children will never know what's possible unless they are encouraged to push the boundaries of their capabilities and to bounce back from adversity and try again when things don't go as planned.

Focus on Possibility

From the time I was very young, my father taught me that anything is possible. He believed in me, and this has made all the difference for me. He used to say, "Do your best, be honest and think positively, and things will work out. It might not be easy, but things will work out."

He taught me the value of persistence and hard work, and so much more. My father's unwavering vision of the glass as half full and never half empty has stuck with me.

We were playing golf together about seven years ago on a beautiful summer day. It was a perfect day. My dad was struggling with Parkinson's disease at the time, but he was out there doing his best and enjoying the fact that he was playing golf. We were having a fantastic time together.

He said, "It doesn't matter how far I can hit the ball. The thing that matters is the fact that I can hit the ball at all."

My dad always focused on the possibilities in the situation at hand and worked to maximize his potential regardless of the obstacles he faced. Why is this important? Because it matters that we always work to hit the ball as far as we can, and it matters that we work to maximize our own unique potential within our given context. It mattered to me because I was able to live fully when I came to understand the importance of hard work, persistence, honesty and positive thinking, and when I internalized the idea of possibility through the lessons my dad taught me. I was able to understand the importance of getting back up and moving forward when faced with challenge. In this way, I moved towards realizing my own potential. The ability to focus on possibility within the context of challenge and to be persistent in this focus is what allows us to move forward and is what defines potential.

Having established a foundation defining resilience, potential and the relationship between the two concepts, let's shift our focus to the seven pillars of resilience for children. I use "pillars" to describe these ideas because the word provides an apt metaphor – building a solid support system that allows a child to ultimately move towards what is possible.

CHAPTER 3

Tolerating Frustration and Managing Emotions: Pillar One

Quinn has his head down on his desk and tears flow from his eyes as he gives up on completing a set of math problems that he considers impossible. The second grader is supposed to complete sixty addition problems within three minutes, but all he can manage is forty-six. "I hate math!" he cries. His teacher is perplexed because she knows he has the conceptual framework to do this work.

Fred is giving a book report in his fourth-grade class. He has prepared for this. He felt confident in the morning before school. Yet, now that he's up in front of the class, he can't remember any of what he read or anything that he planned to say. His mind goes blank, his face turns red and his stomach aches. "Oh no," he thinks, "what am I going to do?" He tries harder, but his mind is still blank. He stands in front of the class, helpless.

Most of us have known children who struggle like Quinn and Fred, or maybe we can relate to the experiences ourselves. The more frustrated these children become, the less they can perform. They're perfectly capable of doing the work, but for some reason fear and dread take over. How can we help these children become more resilient in such situations? What tools can we give them?

Students who can't tolerate frustration and manage their emotions are not positioned to maximize their potential. Building resilience to the stressors they will encounter in school allows students like Fred and Quinn to move forward despite challenges. This will lead to a better chance of both students reaching their full potential.

POTENTIAL: ONE SIZE DOES NOT FIT ALL

It's important to mention that "potential" will likely look very different for both boys because it will depend on many variables. For example, their context is important: what kind of support they have at home, their learning styles and pacing requirements in the classroom. Not all students work at the same pace and not all students learn in the same way. This doesn't mean that one way is better than another, or that students who work faster will achieve more or have more potential. It means that when helping children work to maximize their potential, it's important to consider the many variables at play and tailor the strategies for each child accordingly.

The ability to tolerate frustration and manage emotions is vital in building resilience in children. As demonstrated by both Quinn and Fred, it's possible for a child to get so bogged down in frustration and emotional responses to challenging situations that the child shuts down and can't move forward. Clearly, this can impact performance in school on many levels. Children might give up, get stuck, and begin to internalize the belief that, "It's too hard for me. It's impossible, so why even try?" Once this starts to happen, a child loses belief in her own abilities and in the idea of possibility. This is a sure way to stall a child's ability and desire to work towards what is possible.

We know that school can be, and often will be, challenging. Learning anything for the first time is often daunting for anyone. It's the child's ability to manage the challenge – and not let the challenge manage her – that is so vital to success and the ability to move forward towards ultimate potential. Once children have the skills in place to do this, they are in a much better position to succeed in the classroom within their own unique context. I like to think of a child's collection of coping skills as his toolbox.

As the child adds skills, when he encounters a challenge or obstacle he can rummage in his toolbox and find a tool to help him overcome the challenge. The idea here is that by developing skills and adding tools to their toolboxes, children are amassing vital coping skills to help them navigate the challenges they will inevitably face as they grow into independent, resilient people.

Skills that help kids regulate their emotions and emotional responses, especially when encountering stress, are vital for building resilience. Here's how that might play out for Quinn and Fred:

- Quinn has mastered the concepts to do the work. The question is how to help him access a state of mind and being that will get him into the flow of the assignment without letting his frustration about his pace drive an emotional or reactive response that could cause him to shut down completely and finish even fewer problems. Quinn's toolbox needs skills to help him manage his emotions that he can access when he encounters a challenging situation in or out of the classroom: such skills will help him work more effectively, in a state of relative ease, so he can access the information he already knows to complete the assignment.

- Fred would also certainly benefit from building skills to manage his emotions ahead of time, to put him in a more relaxed state as he prepares for such a presentation, and to manage unexpected anxiety during the presentation. Integrating such skills over time would build resilience in Fred, making him more immune to the feelings of pressure brought on by the presentation.

MANAGING EMOTIONS AND TOLERATING FRUSTRATION IN SPORTS

Playing sports also brings issues of resilience into focus and incorporates broader lessons for life. In coaching young athletes on building a strong mental game, I have seen how vital it is for them to be able to manage their emotions and tolerate frustration. Without these skills, it's difficult for athletes to move beyond obstacles and make progress towards potential, and it's difficult to improve skills and build a strong foundation. Let's consider a few examples.

GREG'S GOLF GAME

Greg is seven years old, and he is learning to play golf. He has been excited about this for some time, but he didn't realize how challenging it could be. Greg wants to be perfect, and in golf there is no such thing as perfection.

After a great lesson with his coach, Greg goes out on the course with his parents to play a few holes. He hits his drive off the tee well and is happy enough with the result. His next shot is less smooth, and Greg is unhappy to say the least. His head is down, he's on the verge of tears and he can't hear his mom and dad explaining that every shot in golf can't be great or even good. Nope, Greg cannot or will not hear it. He wants perfection, despite his limited experience on the course. Armed with these unrealistic expectations for himself, Greg tackles the next shot. When it goes as poorly as the one before it, Greg becomes very emotional. He cries and bangs his club on the ground. When his parents both let him know kindly, but firmly, that this behavior is not acceptable, he becomes sullen and withdrawn. The outward behavior stops, but it's clear that Greg is very upset and shutting down for the round.

What can Greg's parents do? Sure, they could pack it in for the day, but how will that help Greg? What message will that send? Instead, Greg's parents forge on with the round. They offer encouragement by letting Greg know that learning golf takes time and practice. They also tell him to always think about the next shot, not the last shot. They want to instill in Greg the importance of moving forward despite challenge and not giving up when he doesn't do as well as he'd like. In this way, they model the idea of tolerating frustration and managing emotions, especially the expressions of emotions. Greg starts to internalize the importance of persevering through challenge to get to the next level. By the end of the round, Greg is excited again, and he finishes with a huge smile on his face. By sticking with it and not letting his emotions get the best of him, Greg makes progress. This ability to persevere and bounce back from challenge is at the core of resilience that determines what is possible.

ALLY'S TENNIS FRUSTRATION

Ally is a twelve-year-old nationally ranked junior tennis player who has been playing tournaments since the age of eight. On this day, she's losing to someone she has easily beaten many times in the past. Unfortunately, this same scenario has become a trend over the past year. She is becoming highly frustrated with herself and losing her composure both outwardly and inwardly. The more frustrated Ally becomes, the more shots she misses, the more points she loses and the less confidence she has.

How can Ally stop this trend of losing matches she is capable of winning, which is making it impossible for her to realize her potential as a tennis player? Like Greg, Ally needs to learn to better manage her negative emotions, especially during matches.

TOOLS TO HELP ALL SKILL LEVELS

There are specific tools that both Greg and Ally could use to help them build a powerful toolbox of coping techniques and ultimately perform at their best. These tools help with a number of confidence-building and emotional control strategies and are detailed in the action steps at the end of this chapter. It is important to note that the same tools that will benefit Ally will also benefit Greg, even though he's a beginner in his sport and Ally is very experienced. The tools don't just apply to elite athletes, but to anyone who loves a sport and wants to be the best they can be without being held back by their emotions. Ultimately, the idea of tolerating frustration and managing emotions applies across domains and regardless of one's level of play.

Developing skills and adding tools to their toolboxes focused on strategies for tolerating frustration and managing emotions fosters vital coping skills in young athletes. These coping skills will help them to navigate the challenges they will inevitably face in sports and will also help them build resilience in school.

Pillar One Action Steps: Tolerating Frustration and Managing Emotions

Here's a list of strategies that can help a child who is struggling with tolerating frustration or managing emotions in school or in sports. Parents and teachers can get started on some of these right away; others may require individually tailored coaching by a certified professional.

IN THE CLASSROOM

- Help the child access the right state of mind (positive, focused, etc.) to succeed.
- Work with the child to build strategies to regulate emotions.
- Help the child build belief in herself and her abilities.
- Identify the child's learning style; use and tailor teaching strategies accordingly.
- Identify the child's strengths and give the child opportunities to shine by using them.

IN SPORTS

- Help the child manage his expectations for performance (some days will be better than others, but always strive to do your best).
- Help the child learn to tolerate mistakes, while understanding that mistakes will happen – nobody is perfect.
- Find ways for the child to separate performance from self-concept (i.e., build self-esteem).
- Build confidence in the child's skills and proficiency through practice; encourage her to practice effectively. (Remember the Kung Fu instructor: "perfect practice makes perfect.")

- Develop an age-appropriate program to allow the child to master skills while coping with inevitable disappointments along the way.
- Identify potential negative self-talk and make the child aware of it. Explain that such talk may bring down her level of performance.
- Develop affirmations and positive thoughts that the child can integrate into his mental game.

CHAPTER 4

Navigating Friendships and Social Pressures: Pillar Two

Max is a sensitive child who is socially aware and wants to understand why his friends act the way they do and say the things they say. Socially and emotionally, Max is ahead of many of his peers in the way he processes words and actions. While this is an essential skill in life, from the perspective of navigating the social waters of second grade, thinking more deeply on a social/emotional level is not yet as helpful. It sets Max apart from his peers, who think in less abstract and more immediate ways. While peers shrug off a friend's change in an after-school playdate or in recess plans on a given day, Max wants to understand on a much deeper level why these changes occur. He wonders, "Why does my friend say what he says?" and "Why does he act the way he does?" Max is genuinely upset by some behaviors and often feels very sad as a result, whereas most of his peers tend not to notice them and move forward with their day.

    How can we help a child like Max feel better about these situations and navigate through them in a way that enables him to become more resilient? What tools can we offer to help him to better tolerate such situations? Time and maturity are certainly one way to go, along with conversation with a trusted mentor, teacher or parent. Or, we might work with Max on developing skills to manage social stressors and disappointments, which are an inevitable part of school no matter how much we try to protect against them as parents and educators. Encouraging Max to still ask his questions and wonder on this deeper level, while also finding ways to mitigate his emotional responses with tools from his toolbox so he can move beyond disappointment and find resolution to social conflict, are two vital steps we can take.

Dealing with Social Pressures

Being able to tolerate the ups and downs of social relationships during the elementary years is essential to children's ability to bounce back from the inevitable disappointments they will face in school, socially and otherwise. No child is immune to the many challenges that come up in school. Developing coping strategies to handle such social challenges in the moment and over the long term makes all the difference and enables children to develop a more complete sense of themselves and their ability to keep moving forward despite challenge.

Friendships can be somewhat fleeting in these years as children develop a sense of what defines them. And of course, what defines an elementary student is sure to change numerous times over the years. Tools related to emotional self-regulation, social awareness and self-awareness can be very useful in such situations. These tools help children to not overreact and to better understand how their own behavior and words impact others, and how the behavior and words of others impact them. Adding these to the toolboxes of young children as they begin the process of navigating social situations is not only invaluable – it is essential. Having tools to negotiate potentially hurtful and confusing social experiences in school provides kids with a sense of empowerment through a greater sense of themselves, particularly within the context of social situations.

By helping kids to build these skills of emotional self-regulation, social awareness and self-awareness, we are helping them to become more resilient. And within this context of resilience, we are helping them to move closer to their personal potential for navigating friendships and social pressures by creating a firm launchpad for them to understand more not only about themselves, but also about others. These skills are also vital in helping kids to further develop a sense of empathy and compassion for those around them, and in turn to be accepting and understanding of individual differences inevitably present among classmates and friends.

Accepting Individual Differences

Individual differences are a part of life, and the ability to accept and embrace such differences among peers in school is a vital skill that will help a child have a smoother time socially. Children who "stand out" socially or otherwise quickly learn what individual differences mean. This lesson fosters a sense of resilience early if the child develops the tools to regulate her response to how others react to the difference. Children who develop tools to regulate their response to others develop the capacity to be resilient in the face of negative and unkind responses from peers, and also become more tolerant of others who are different in some way. Let's look at how this might play out.

Adam: Resisting Taunts of Others

Adam is a kindergartener who likes a football team from another city that is not the team favored by most kids in his school. When Adam wears a team jersey or hat to school, he is bullied and taunted because nobody else likes that team. One day on the playground, an older boy grabs Adam's hat off his head, throws it in a puddle and starts laughing. Adam is crushed. "Why would a bigger boy do that to me?" he wonders. At home, he explains to his mother what happened at school that day. "Why can't I like this other team?" he asks her through his tears. The answer is that the other kids clearly have difficulty accepting this slice of individual difference that Adam brings into their worlds by choosing a "different" team.

While it seems like a simple example, this experience is quite profound for Adam. The taunting and bullying continue for three years as Adam continues to wear his team's gear because it is special to him – it was a gift from his uncle. Adam continues to wear the hat and the kids continue to taunt him. Helping Adam add tools to his toolbox that allow him to better cope with the taunts is vital during these years. An important part of the process is helping Adam understand that the other children's opinions don't matter. As Adam learns to cope with the taunts, he finds that over time they don't bother him as much. Instead of ending up in tears on the playground, he is learning to take a step back and recognize that what the other kids say does not matter in the bigger scope of things. As a result, he takes the taunts less personally. In this way, Adam becomes more resilient and frees up space within himself to continue moving forward on his own path and not remain bogged down in the unkind and mean behavior of some of those around him. At the same time, Adam develops a great deal of empathy for other kids who are struggling through similar experiences. Although unpleasant and not easy, Adam's struggle helps him develop a robust toolbox for coping with the inevitable pressures and challenges of life in a positive way.

Adam's story in many ways reminds me of my own struggle with being different in my early school years, because of the social challenges my hydrocephalus presented. For example, I had to wear a hockey helmet while ice-skating with my class long before hockey helmets were cool. Nobody wore helmets back then. It was humiliating as I skated around and heard my peers snickering and laughing. I was just happy to be out there skating, and I was lucky I could, given the medical challenges I had going on and the number of brain surgeries I had already undergone. Yet, the sneers and the taunts still hurt, regardless of my underlying appreciation of the fact that I could be skating at all.

While I was not taught any specific tools for managing how this affected me, I did pick up over time that I gained power by ignoring what others said and how they acted towards me, and not letting on how much it hurt. Still, over time this type of passive approach can be quite exhausting, draining and demoralizing. Looking back, having a set of specific tools that I could have used to help me cope on both an emotional and a cognitive level would have been so useful. I was fortunate in that I had a lot of support at home, and I had many close friends who did not laugh, but rather acted as if there was nothing different about my helmet and the other things that made me stand out in those early years. This helped me to develop a thicker skin and to cope.

Elliot: Social Pressure in Sports

Elliot is eight years old and loves baseball. In fact, he loves baseball so much that it is almost all he talks about, and all he wants to do in his free time is play baseball. Yet, as the season approaches, Elliot is increasingly concerned by what others think of him on the field. If he makes a mistake, he immediately starts to cry and wants to quit for the day. If he strikes out, he starts to obsess about what his teammates, coach and parents think of him. Suddenly, his love of the game is overshadowed by his developing and somewhat overpowering self-consciousness about what others think. It's hard to tell what's driving this concern, but it is distracting him from his love of baseball and is also affecting his performance in a negative way. Those around him notice the change in Elliot: he is no longer the carefree little boy with a love and talent for baseball.

As with the examples discussed earlier, Elliot would certainly benefit from tools to help him regulate his emotional responses in a more positive way on the baseball field. Developing such tools and integrating them into his way of being will help Elliot to become more resilient to the inevitable ups and downs of playing sports. We don't always have our best day, regardless of what we're doing, and the sooner young kids understand and live this idea, the faster they will maximize their potential within the context of their sport.

We might also work with Elliot to manage his underlying fear of failure and high expectations for himself on the baseball field. It's clear that an underlying fear of failure combined with high expectations can damage one's confidence. Addressing these issues with him in a developmentally appropriate way will likely help Elliot to cope and build resilience in baseball and in life. For example, he'll realize that he can walk away knowing he didn't have his best day, but that he can come back next time and do better. The experience won't derail him, but rather it will make him stronger and more resilient on the baseball field, in school and beyond. How the child responds to such experiences both inwardly and outwardly is truly what makes all the difference.

Julia: Playing for Herself or for Others?

Julia is ten years old and plays tennis competitively, mostly in club events close to home. She is talented but does not particularly like to practice; in fact, she gets angry every time her father suggests she do so. When she plays tennis with her father, she often doesn't give her best because in truth, she would rather be doing something else. Julia continues to play because her friends play, her family plays and she likes to win trophies. But most of the time her heart is not in it, and this is becoming more and more obvious to those around her. Playing when she would rather not play takes the joy out of the game for Julia and for her tennis partners and opponents. Who wants to play with someone who is grumpy and would rather be somewhere else? Julia needs help reconnecting with her early love of tennis and fostering resilience in the sport. Without these two ingredients, she will not move towards her potential as a tennis player.

Ultimately, helping Julia to answer the question of why she continues to play tennis is vital, along with providing her with tools to manage the social expectations related to tennis that have become so much a part of the mix for her. If Julia plays to please those around her, chances are that these social influences will not sustain her as a tennis player and will not lead her towards her potential. The question that must be answered becomes, who is Julia playing tennis for in the first place? Does she play for herself or does she play for all those around her? Once she can answer this question, she can move on to the next step of either re-engaging with tennis or finding an alternative sport, even if she eventually misses tennis and comes back to it. The social influences in Julia's life have an impact on her tennis and the fact that she continues to play.

Pillar Two Action Steps: Navigating Friendships and Social Pressures

Here's a list of strategies that can help a child who is struggling with navigating friendships and social pressures in school or in sports. Parents and teachers can get started on some of these right away; others may require individually tailored coaching by a certified professional.

IN THE CLASSROOM

- Help the child develop coping skills to manage social pressures and disappointments while encouraging him to still wonder and think deeply about his questions.
- Work with the child on emotional self-regulation and self-awareness skills.
- Teach the child self-monitoring behaviors: "How does your behavior impact others? How does the behavior of others impact you?"
- Work with the child on proactive problem-solving skills.
- Teach the importance of tolerating and appreciating individual differences.
- Show the child that there's power in ignoring taunts and negative comments.

IN SPORTS

- Work with the child on coping skills to manage social pressures and disappointments.
- Work with the child on emotional self-regulation and self-awareness skills.

- Emphasize the importance of persistence.
- Help the child reconnect with her love of the sport.
- Help the child manage expectations; remind him that nobody is perfect.
- Address fear of failure by managing expectations and the need to be perfect.
- Help the child to manage social pressures and influences; remind her that what's important is what she thinks of herself, not what others think of her.

CHAPTER 5

Sustaining Focus and Attention: Pillar Three

Tim is a fifth grader who has decided that this is the year he will make the honor roll. All his friends are on the honor roll, but he has never made it. Tim knows that to succeed, he will need to stay focused on his goal and be diligent with each individual assignment. But Tim has a tendency to get easily distracted from his schoolwork, which makes it difficult to do his best. He spends time after school doing anything but homework, and by the time he sits down to get it done, it's almost time for bed. Thus, he's rushed and rarely puts in his best effort. No matter how much his parents remind him to do his work, Tim isn't able to make it happen.

But now that he's decided to make the honor roll, Tim's outlook changes. He believes he is smart and that he can do this. Fortunately, Tim's parents and teachers also believe in him and his ability to make the honor roll. They support him by filling his toolbox with strategies to strengthen his overall focus and attention and to help him cope when things are hard. They also help Tim set realistic and achievable goals to keep him on track to reach his bigger objective of making the honor roll.

SETTING A GOAL

When a child struggles to maintain focus on daily tasks related to school and beyond, it takes away from his ability to perform up to potential. At the same time, this can be distracting to other children in the classroom and can detract from the teacher's ability to teach a lesson or make a point. In many ways, this ability to focus on specific goals while keeping a larger goal in mind has a distinct developmental component and takes time to evolve for many children. Some have an inherently easier time with focus, attention and organization from the outset. For those who need extra support in this domain in order to live up to their potential, many useful tools exist. The foundation for honing this ability to focus can be fostered by introducing and integrating such tools during the elementary school years.

Why is the child who can stay focused on a single task and a larger goal more resilient? For one thing, a focused child is likely more self-directed and able to navigate more independently through daily tasks. Focus, particularly on a longer-term goal, in many ways eliminates distraction and the emphasis on immediate gratification, which in turn fosters the idea that success takes work and persistence. This reinforces the idea that reaching goals takes focus, so there is a synergy here. As children practice and internalize this idea over time, they become more resilient to the ups and downs of life. With the end goal in mind, it becomes easier to try another tactic if the first approach does not work. Additionally, goals foster forward motion.

An optimistic outlook that progress towards a goal is possible fosters an understanding that success in accomplishing goals is a process: reaching a larger goal often requires meeting several smaller goals along the way. Understanding this idea while developing the persistence to follow through on a larger goal is a powerful lesson and one that often takes some time to learn.

REX: READING BETTER THROUGH PRACTICE AND PERSISTENCE

Rex didn't like to read in first grade and second grade, but now that he's in third grade he wants to improve his reading skills so that he can read advanced books about topics that interest him. He has suddenly realized that if he improves enough through practice and persistence, he can read the new Star Wars books in his classroom all on his own. His passion for all things Star Wars drives Rex to practice reading every day. He does all the exercises his teacher suggests and reads aloud every night. Rex benefits from these extra tools in his toolbox, which help with the technical aspects of reading and decoding, along with tools to increase focus and attention to help him cope with the inevitable frustration he encounters in the process of becoming a stronger reader. By not giving up when faced with challenge, Rex makes progress and is, in time, reading the Star Wars books he wants to read.

Rex also benefits greatly from tools to help him believe in himself and his ability to become a better reader. Helping children to believe in their own abilities, whether in the classroom or on the playing field, is a central element of building resilience and maximizing potential over time.

LEARNING REQUIRES RESILIENCE

Learning doesn't happen in a straight line. There is forward progress, and then often some stagnation or steps back before true progress is made. This is a natural part of the process of learning, whether in the classroom or on the playing field.

By practicing and integrating a higher level of focus on both small and large goals over time, children become more resilient to the inevitable ups and downs, and starts and stops, in the process of learning. It is the ability to stay in the process in the moment and not give up over the longer haul that fosters resilience, while helping children move towards their own unique potential. It is also important to note here that this process will never look the same for two children because of individual contexts, experiences and abilities.

BILL: FOCUS AND ATTENTION IN SPORTS

Bill is a fourth grader who wants to make the swim team. The problem is, he does not want to practice his strokes. Somehow, he thinks his times will improve magically on their own without extra practice. His parents don't want to nag him but they're bracing themselves for his inevitable disappointment, because the truth is that without practice, Bill is not going to make the swim team.

Unfortunately, Bill doesn't make the connection between his dream of being on the swim team and the idea of setting goals and working hard to achieve his goals. Bill would benefit from tools to help him define his overall goal (i.e., to make the swim team), while coming up with smaller, more immediate goals to help him get there. Further, he would benefit from a clear road map for getting from point A (i.e., where he is now) to point B (i.e., a member of the swim team). Bill will also benefit from tools to help him manage his emotional response to practice. Self-regulating in this way would essentially make practice feel easier or more manageable by creating a state of flow and ultimately helping him to feel more at ease in the water. As this happens, Bill will be more drawn to practice because it won't feel so hard. The more he practices, the more he will improve. These self-regulation skills will not only help Bill flourish in the water, but also in the classroom, in his friendships and beyond.

At the same time, an adult Bill trusts can explain, in an age-appropriate manner, the benefits of focus, setting goals and working towards those goals in practice. This can instill in Bill the reality that he will not progress as a swimmer without clear goals, focus and practice. It's as simple as that. Focusing on single tasks and larger goals while tolerating stress and managing emotions are central skills in the development of resilience and the ability to maximize potential.

Jonathan: Total Commitment to a Goal

Jonathan is 11 years old and a fifth grader. He has been doing Kung Fu for three years and loves the sport. His goal is to earn his black belt in the next two years. By nature, learning Kung Fu is a long process that requires focus, attention and the ability to make a long-term commitment to the process. The latter is the underlying key to success in Kung Fu.

In order for Jonathan to achieve his black belt in the next two years, he needs a plan. The first step is to work with his Kung Fu instructor to outline the exact steps he needs to complete to get his black belt. The next step is to make an agreement with himself that he will go to every practice unless he is sick or on vacation. Jonathan knows that without total commitment to his goal, he will likely not achieve it.

Kung Fu is a sport that fosters a child's ability to self-regulate, focus and attend to the task at hand and often a larger goal (i.e., achieving a black belt in a certain time frame). By committing to weekly practice in Kung Fu, a child fills his toolbox with important skills for success that apply in other aspects of life as well. On top of this, trusted adults can work with Jonathan to build other tools that will help strengthen the existing benefits of his Kung Fu practice, such as mastering emotions, building confidence, and reframing negative self-talk. These are listed in more detail in the action steps at the end of the chapter.

By practicing and integrating these skills, Jonathan will bolster his toolbox with valuable tools to use across domains over the long term. The foundation is in place for meeting his goal if he stays committed and focused.

Coping with Distraction

The ability to cope with distraction is vital for success both in the classroom and in sports and athletic performance. Key steps in the ability to cope successfully with distraction include the following:

- Recognizing that you are off task
- Refocusing on what is relevant in terms of the task
- Regrouping by stopping and getting back on task

As noted, focus is a developmental skill that takes time to develop fully, but it can be fostered from a young age by giving children tools that can be honed over time. The more a child can stay focused on the task at hand and the larger goal, the more resilient he or she becomes to the inevitable ups and downs of the process of getting from point A to point B. When the going gets tough, children who can get back up and continue moving forward will be more likely to maximize their unique potential.

Pillar Three Action Steps: Sustaining Focus and Attention

Here's a list of strategies that can help a child who is struggling with sustaining focus and attention in school or in sports. Parents and teachers can get started on some of these right away; others may require individually tailored coaching by a certified professional.

In the Classroom

- Help the child set attainable and manageable goals.
- Reinforce the importance of giving one's best effort.
- Help the child see the importance of finishing what one starts.
- Teach strategies for building focus on goals and avoiding distraction.
- Manage self-talk by addressing negative statements and replacing them with positive affirmation.
- Give the child tools to improve skills in the areas where he is also trying to focus; e.g., reading exercises if he needs to focus on reading.
- Help the child believe in her own abilities.

In Sports

- Work with the child to establish short- and long-term goals.
- Create routines for meeting goals.
- Show the child that mastering one skill at a time builds confidence.
- Help the child to master emotions by focusing on the positive and looking forward, not backward.

- Teach the child to reframe negative self-talk, for example by keeping a log of negative remarks and coming up with alternative, more productive self-talk.
- Teach strategies for avoiding distraction.

CHAPTER 6

Developing Courage: Pillar Four

Toby is waiting for his turn to come out on stage in the third-grade play. He's listening to his classmates who are in Act One, but he barely hears anything they're saying. Small beads of sweat pop out on his forehead, his vision is a little funny and his stomach hurts. His turn in Act Two is coming up soon.

While some children thrive on performing in school plays, Toby would rather go to the dentist to get a cavity filled than stand up on stage and "perform." For last year's play he memorized his lines, but when he was on stage and it was his turn to speak nothing came out when he opened his mouth. He simply could not get the words out during the play, and it was embarrassing to say the least. So, Toby has been dreading this moment for weeks.

But this time, Toby surprises himself. He walks out on stage when the curtain goes up. While he still feels those beads of sweat, somehow he finds it within himself to say his lines at the right time. And guess what! He makes it through the entire second act without missing a beat. Toby is surprised, relieved and very happy. By pushing himself to face his fear and walk out on stage when all he wanted to do was run from the building, he proves to himself that he is stronger than his fear and more capable than he believes. The many tools Toby has learned during the year, which help him to better tolerate stressful situations, also bolster his confidence and belief that he can remember his lines and say them at the right time in front of the audience.

This is an important early lesson. If he had stayed in his comfort zone and off the stage, Toby would never have known what was possible for him, and he could have remained stagnant. Instead, he showed courage and went on stage despite his nervousness. Toby will use these tools many times moving forward through school.

Peter: Willing to Try and "Fail"

Peter knows the math problem on the board seems hard and he isn't sure that he can do it, especially in front of his class. Yet, when the teacher asks for a volunteer, he shoots his hand in the air, takes a deep breath and walks to the front of the room to attempt this problem. Sure enough, it proves to be a bit complex and he doesn't complete it correctly. Yet, he doesn't feel bad. He has tried his best and he knows it. Peter is able to channel this reality into the idea that he will simply practice problems like this and the next time he has the chance, he'll try again.

Peter wasn't always this willing and able to accept "failure." But the adults in his life made sure he understood that if he never tried things, he would not make the progress he wanted to make. They provided him with strategies and tools for his toolbox that helped him develop skills in this area. Peter learned early on to view "failure" as an opportunity rather than an obstacle; now he has the courage to fail and learn from it.

Caroline: Moving Forward Despite Fear

Caroline is standing at one end of the swaying suspension bridge that her classmates just walked across on a school field trip. The wind is blowing and the bridge is moving fast. The gully below looks cold and dark. She wants to start walking across like her classmates just did without a thought. But Caroline is terrified and she can't seem to move no matter how much she wants to; her legs have turned into cement blocks. Finally, after what seems like hours, one of Caroline's teachers comes back across the bridge to encourage her to join her class on the other side. After several minutes of coaxing, Caroline feels comfortable enough to move forward with her teacher close behind offering encouragement and support.

By crossing the bridge, Caroline is building her courage and overcoming her fear of heights, with her teacher's support. It is the courage to overcome and move forward despite fear that builds resilience.

Emma: Making a Change

Emma is a ten-year-old fourth grader who's a very bright and historically happy student. Yet, in the past year, she has become bored at school and is struggling to stay engaged in learning, likely because her learning style doesn't match her current school environment. She isn't motivated and she feels beaten down. Emma needs a change, but what's the next step? Around this time, her mother finds out about an alternative, hybrid school model that is part home school and part classroom-based. This seems like just what Emma needs to reinvigorate her love of learning. Despite some initial hesitation about making such a big change and embarking on an unchartered course with so many unknowns, they take the leap.

Making this change takes courage, but it pays off. Emma's entire view of learning shifts back to one of excitement and vitality. She can't wait to see what each new day has to offer. She is thriving on the independence embedded in the new model of learning, and this is fostering her sense of intrinsic motivation. Emma is learning to take charge of her education through goal-setting and persistence. Sometimes, harnessing our courage, facing the unknown and making a change despite uncertainty opens doors and possibilities we never knew existed.

Taking a risk and doing something that feels scary can be an important component of propelling a child forward and unlocking her potential. A child's belief in himself and his ability to succeed can become clouded by fear of risk or moving out of his comfort zone. Children who truly believe they can succeed are able to step outside of their comfort zone and tolerate a degree of risk that things won't go perfectly. This is true courage.

We know that all children do not think in the same way. Sure, they may have the same conceptual ideas in mind, but the way they make sense of the world and new concepts both in school and out of school differs greatly. It takes courage to break free from the status quo and come up with your own ideas for how to do things. It is important to encourage children to embrace the idea of acting courageously in ways that makes sense for them by filling their toolbox with tools specific to their needs and personalities.

LEARNING TAKES COURAGE

I was afraid to ride my bike without training wheels as a young girl, yet after a lot of trial and error, I mastered it – on the flat. Then I had to go down a hill for the first time, and the same fear set in. I had to build courage and mastery all over again. Eventually, after many rounds of trial and error, I did it. Ironically, biking became a longtime passion for me, and it has brought me lots of joy. Without the courage to overcome my fear, I would have never experienced this slice of joy.

As the example of learning to ride a bike shows, learning takes courage. This is true whether in the classroom, on a field trip or on the playing field. Courage allows children to try new things. It gives them the space to fail and to try again and provides the foundation for taking risks, thinking out of the box and overcoming fear. To build resilience and maximize potential, a child must have the courage to try. Even if something seems scary, overwhelming or out of reach, children must have the courage to take the first step forward. Similarly, they need to have the courage to get up and try again if at first things do not go as planned, and to keep trying no matter how many attempts it takes to accomplish a goal. While this is not always easy, and in fact is often quite difficult, it is a vital aspect of building resilience and creating a foundation for success in school and beyond.

Developing the Courage to Try and the Courage to Fail

How does a child develop courage? Here are some examples: by overcoming fear, by trying new things and by pushing limits backed by encouragement and support. These experiences are especially important early in life. Think about children who are afraid of everything. They need encouragement to try new things, and only through consistent encouragement can they overcome fear and become more courageous. Why is it important to try? Because if children don't try, they will never know what is possible. And if children never know what is possible, or at least imagine what is possible, it is likely that they will remain stuck or at the very least miss out on what could have been, crippled by fear and living in regret.

Just as it is important to try, it is important to fail. Why? Because failure builds resilience. If things are too easy for a child and she never learns to try again, it will only hurt her in the long run. It takes courage to make mistakes. It's important to learn from experiences that don't go as hoped or planned, but moving beyond failure with courage is the key for future success. It is through this process of having the courage to fail, get back up again and move forward that we can help children build a toolbox that will make them resilient to life's challenges.

This is important because by staying in their comfort zone, children may never know what is possible and may remain stagnant. These children may never experience the opportunity to access and live their potential. Sometimes risk is an important component for propelling children forward and unlocking their potential. Sometimes a child's belief in himself and his ability to succeed becomes clouded by a fear of risk and a fear of moving beyond his comfort zone. Children who truly believe in their ability to succeed are able to step outside of their comfort zone and tolerate a degree of risk without a guarantee that things will work out. This is true courage.

Building skills in emotional awareness and self-regulation, along with stress tolerance, helps children find the courage to try and then try again when things don't go as planned the first time around. These tools give children confidence and belief in self to take steps forward even without knowing where they are going. By adding these specific tools to a child's toolbox, the child develops confidence and belief in self along with the courage to understand that it is okay to try again; in fact, it is important to try again so as not to lose out on opportunities. This is an important early lesson.

Lenny and Alex: Courage in Sports

Ten-year-old Lenny is standing in the dugout waiting for his turn at bat during the first playoff game of the season. He's terrified. His legs feel like rubber bands and his hands are shaking so much that he drops his bat every time he tries to pick it up. Lenny doesn't want to go up to bat and face the pitcher who hit him hard in the back with a pitch in last week's game. Getting hit hurt, but more than the pain, the experience of getting hit by a pitch scared Lenny. For many kids, this fear often dissipates when a pitch does hit them and they realize they are still okay. But for Lenny, getting hit scared him to the point that he was not sure he wanted to play baseball anymore.

For now, though, he is playing and he needs to go up to bat so he doesn't let his team down. His teammates yell encouragement and Lenny takes his place in the batter's box. While he strikes out quickly and is a bit disappointed, he is also relieved that he didn't let his team down by not even trying. Whether Lenny continues to play baseball next year doesn't matter. What matters is that he harnessed his inner strength in that moment and found the courage to bat. In the process, he proved to himself that he was stronger than his fear.

Making the transition from the ball machine to the less predictable kid pitch is a rite of passage for all young Little League baseball players. Alex, also ten, is apprehensive about this transition, and this is evident during his first couple of times at the plate with another kid pitching to him. Like Lenny, he's afraid of getting hit, and he doesn't want to strike out and look stupid in front of his teammates and family. But over time he does get hit, and he does strike out. Alex's apprehension about not doing well doesn't prevent the outcome he most fears.

Yet, with the addition of some tools to his toolbox, Alex comes to understand that striking out – and even getting hit by pitches – is a real part of mastering this new level of baseball. These tools include coaching on batting technique as well as specialized training to build resilience and master skills of self-regulation. Experience and maturity also help. With more time and practice, Alex reframes his anxious outlook and uses his new skills to calm his mind and body each time he comes to bat. If he gets a hit, great. If he doesn't, it's okay. Alex believes that each time he comes to bat, he has a chance to make the best hit of his life. He uses the tools in his toolbox to accept the outcome of his at-bat – good or bad. In this way, he can feel successful regardless of where the ball lands.

Helping Children Build Courage

It's important for children to have the courage to try again if things don't work out on the first attempt. This is a central idea in their ability to believe in themselves and their ability to overcome challenge. Among other things, courage builds resilience and persistence, both of which help children to keep moving forward despite challenge. How do children develop this kind of courage? I would argue that they develop it when, as young children, they are encouraged to try again when things do not go as planned the first time, or to try something new, different or even scary. We can foster courage to unlock potential by encouraging children to take risks and by encouraging them to push the limits of their comfort zones.

Most importantly, parents and teachers can show kids how to do this by believing in them and what they are capable of. Ultimately, it takes courage to keep moving forward when things feel hard and when those around you do not believe in you or your ability to succeed. When we show children that we believe in them through encouragement and example, success becomes attainable and children start to believe in their own abilities and possibilities.

Pillar Four Action Steps: Developing Courage

Here's a list of strategies that can help a child who is struggling with developing courage in school or in sports. Parents and teachers can get started on some of these right away; others may require individually tailored coaching by a certified professional.

In the Classroom

- Encourage the child to face her fears.
- Encourage the child to push himself beyond his comfort zone – to move forward despite fear.
- Encourage the child to try new things in order to see what is possible.
- Help the child develop the courage to fail.
- Encourage the child to try again.
- Give children tools specific to their needs and personalities that encourage them to embrace the idea of acting courageously in ways that makes sense for them.
- Teach the child strategies for emotional awareness, self-regulation and stress tolerance.

In Sports

- Teach the child how to manage expectations.
- Help the child to address fear of failure.
- Encourage the child to take risks.

- Push the child beyond her comfort zone so she has an opportunity to move forward despite fear.
- Coach children on technique so they can master what they can control and better handle what they can't control (e.g., batting technique will help them hit better, although it won't prevent them from getting hit by a pitch).

CHAPTER 7

Building Motivation: Pillar Five

I remember sitting for hours in fourth grade reading books and working on book reports. Sure, I probably wanted to be doing other things that were more fun, but I also had an inner drive to do my best on my schoolwork. By nature, I was motivated from the inside out to do most things, and I wanted to get things done the way they needed to be done even when it wasn't easy. Perhaps this was because of the medical challenges I faced, which caused me to miss a lot of school. I did a lot of starting, stopping and catching up, and this made some of the most basic and mundane tasks more difficult. My internal motivation might also have come from what my dad and mom taught me at home: "Always do your best no matter what, because nobody can take that away from you." It was likely a combination of factors that drove my early motivation. What I do know for sure is that the motivation to get things done, to keep moving forward even when things are hard or overwhelming, stuck with me over time and opened up some great opportunities that might not have been possible otherwise.

MOTIVATION AND RESILIENCE

Motivation is a central concept in building resilience and maximizing potential. There are two types of motivation, intrinsic and extrinsic:

- Intrinsic motivation comes from the inside out and develops through the process of trial and error, through early processes of discovery of self and how we fit in. Intrinsic motivation evolves over time as kids develop. It's an important part of how we come to recognize and maximize our own sense of potential and possibility.

- Extrinsic motivation is fostered from the outside in, driven by external reward or praise.

While extrinsic motivation can be a useful tool in propelling children forward towards goals and potential, I believe that intrinsic motivation is a more powerful long-term driver of resilience and potential.

TIM: FROM EXTRINSIC TO INTRINSIC MOTIVATION

Tim, a fifth grader, has been motivated to read from an early age. At first his motivation was extrinsic, driven by external rewards such as earning a teacher's praise or points for the class reading challenge. Yet, the process of reading every day for those rewards sparked a true love of reading for him that quickly became intrinsically motivated. Tim developed an authentic love for reading that has grown over time and serves him well in school. He's motivated to read about topics that interest him and are relevant to his life, most notably dogs and sports. The point here is that what begins as extrinsic motivation can develop into intrinsic motivation over time.

Both intrinsic and extrinsic motivation are important for children, but as noted above, intrinsic motivation tends to offer longer-term benefits for a child since it is not dependent on anyone except the child.

HELPING CHILDREN CULTIVATE INTRINSIC MOTIVATION

Intrinsic motivation is an important factor in reaching goals, fostering resilience and moving towards true potential. Motivation is at the very essence of resilience – the ability to get up and move forward despite challenge. Without an inner desire, children are less likely to find it within themselves to move forward after a setback or challenge.

Fostering and encouraging intrinsic motivation in children from an early age is very important.

Intrinsic motivation comes more naturally to some children than to others, and it can take time to develop. Often, it's a result of time, experience and the normative developmental process. It's not uncommon for younger children to be motivated purely by external reward, such as doing chores for a Lego toy or a piece of candy.

What might help children cultivate intrinsic motivation? Here are some strategies:

- Provide them with tools to set goals and to identify and develop their interests and strengths.
- Help them focus on the reasons why they want to do well.
- Give children the opportunity to observe friends and peers working hard and achieving success at a sport or other activity; they will see intrinsic motivation in action.
- Teachers can engage and draw students out in a way that's instructive and fun.
- As a parent, model intrinsic motivation for your children to observe in your own actions.

Experiencing success and failure can also be powerful intrinsic motivators for children. For most people, working hard and achieving good results provides encouragement to continue working hard in order to continue achieving good – or even better – results. Through understanding what we want and what it will take to get there from the inside out (i.e., intrinsic motivators), we can work towards realizing our potential. Following are some case studies showing why intrinsic motivation matters in maximizing potential.

Liz: The Problem with Extrinsic Motivation Alone

Liz seemed to have everything going for her through elementary, middle and high school. She was pretty and popular, had the best grades, and was the best at sports. Everything she touched seemed to turn to gold. But now that she's in college, she is struggling. Suddenly, everything seems difficult – maintaining good grades, picking courses, making friends, keeping things organized … and the list goes on. The reality is that Liz isn't used to doing these things by herself. She is overwhelmed and uncertain about how to stay on course.

On her own and away from the watchful and reinforcing eye of her parents and childhood community, Liz needs to use her internal compass to reinforce her own ideas and sense of direction for how to use her broad range of talents. The problem is that Liz can't access that internal compass because she didn't develop it early in life. She was always extrinsically motivated, and without the constant reinforcement from those around her now that she's in college, Liz is lost and adrift in a world of too many possibilities and temptations. Despite her earlier successes, the constant external validation she received kept her from developing a sense of direction and belief in herself.

Liz would benefit from tools to help her identify and internalize her strengths and to set goals with specific action steps. She would also benefit from basic life skills training to help her manage living away from home for the first time. Without such tools in place, it will be difficult for Liz to develop into a resilient and self-directed young adult.

Children who rely too heavily on extrinsic or external motivation over time will likely not be as resilient when facing life's inevitable challenges and disappointments as those who develop intrinsic motivation early on. Fostering intrinsic motivation from an early age by providing tools and strategies is vital. If a child does not possess the inner compass that comes along with strong intrinsic motivation to guide them forward, reaching full potential will prove that much more challenging.

Next is an example of a child who might have been headed in the same direction if the adults in his life hadn't made sure he got the tools he needed.

Sal: Skills Training for Intrinsic Motivation

Sal is a bright nine-year-old student, yet when faced with free time or tasked with defining his own direction, he just can't seem to move forward without external direction at every turn. Ask Sal to work independently and he asks what to do. Ask him to complete a free write and he asks what to write about. He has free time to play on his own and he asks someone to play with him. There seems to be a void when it comes to being able to access his internal compass and engage independently. This makes it challenging for him to stick with things in and out of the classroom. It also impacts his level of motivation, particularly his intrinsic motivation. His parents notice this and arrange for him to get help. The positive news is that six weeks of specific skills training in self-regulation and emotion management let Sal fill his toolbox with tools to strengthen these skills. Now, Sal is able to pick a direction, engage more successfully and move forward independently. This shift is amazingly powerful for Sal as it allows him to access his internal compass and discover his passions. His sense of intrinsic motivation is much stronger and he regularly engages in activities he loves without constant external prodding. This new outlook allows Sal to live more in line with his natural potential.

Intrinsically motivated students want to learn for the sake of learning; they are driven by passion and they understand the importance and value of hard work for mastering skills over the long term. This type of passion in learning takes time, and it is important to lay the groundwork in the early elementary and middle school years. Another critical point here is the idea of rewarding effort as opposed to ability in the younger student.

Keeping things fun and engaging is critical, particularly for elementary students. Otherwise, they may give up on engaging at all.

Peggy: An Athlete's Motivation

Intrinsic motivation is equally important for young athletes if they are going to thrive. Peggy is a ten-year-old junior triathlete. After Peggy learned to ride a bike, her mom said, "You can swim, run and bike. It's time to try a triathlon." Peggy had never heard of a triathlon, but was immediately intrigued by an event where she could do three of her favorite activities. She asked her mom to sign her up for one, and the rest is history. Peggy has been competing in junior triathlons ever since.

It's interesting to note that Peggy tried her first triathlon simply because it appealed to her interest in swimming, running and biking. As discussed earlier in this chapter, identifying and developing interests and strengths is one way to help develop intrinsic motivation. It was only after competing for a while that Peggy realized how much she loves competition and the challenge it presents. So, now Peggy is motivated by the sense of accomplishment that comes from finishing races and by the fun she has while racing, the friends she has made and the fitness that comes with competing in triathlons. Peggy's motivation to compete is strengthened by her mother's belief in her ability and in what is possible for her in triathlons and beyond. Having such an important person in her life believe in her fuels Peggy's own belief in herself, and together these factors build on Peggy's underlying resilience and ability to manage challenge as it arises, in addition to her inner drive to set more goals and achieve them in a meaningful way.

Tennis, My Dad, and Me

I was motivated to play tennis as a child because I loved to play and because I knew from early on that my ability to play was a gift, given the medical challenges I faced. I wanted to play because I *could* play, and this benefited me in all areas of my life by making me more resilient physically and mentally. I could not take my ability to play tennis for granted. This lesson stuck with me into adulthood, and I do my best to pass it along to my own children – we can't take our physical abilities for granted, as being out there playing is a gift in itself, which we must take care of and nurture over time.

I didn't always win, and those moments were ones where I was intrinsically motivated and just happy to be out there playing. For me, this was as good as a trophy. Of course, the times when I did win and receive a trophy also felt great and reinforced my desire to play. This is an example of how extrinsic motivators (a trophy) can complement intrinsic motivation (love of playing) and in some instances, strengthen it. But my reality was that the victories were generally not what fueled my desire to play tennis. Rather, it was an intrinsic love of the game that drove me onto the court. My strong relationship with my father and our shared love of tennis strengthened my desire to play even more, as did many other supportive adults in my life who also played tennis. Ultimately, these relationships made me more resilient by providing me with a fundamental belief in myself and my abilities, win or lose. This helped me to develop strengths both on and off the tennis court. If we think about it, the same principles apply when children are motivated to make a sports team, learn a new sport, take up an instrument, learn a language or get good grades, among many other things.

When a child can stay motivated and engaged – both intrinsically and extrinsically – in a process despite challenge, this fosters resilience over time. Identifying and nurturing the ideas and activities that motivate children in school, sports and all aspects of life is a key to building resilience and potential.

Pillar Five Action Steps: Building Motivation

Here's a list of strategies that can help a child who is struggling with building motivation in school or in sports. Parents and teachers can get started on some of these right away; others may require individually tailored coaching by a certified professional.

In the Classroom

- Identify whether the child's motivational tendencies are more intrinsic or extrinsic.
- Foster motivation by discovering and encouraging the child's passions.
- Encourage children to discover and use their strengths.
- Provide opportunities for the child to learn by modeling those around him.
- Encourage engagement through example; give the child an opportunity to witness others engaged in an activity.
- Reward effort as opposed to ability in younger students.

In Sports

- Identify whether the child's motivational tendencies are more intrinsic or extrinsic.
- Foster intrinsic motivations by allowing the child to experiment with different sports in order to discover her true interests.
- Encourage the child to focus on his love of the game.

- Acknowledge the child's sense of accomplishment and make her feel good about it.
- Give the child the opportunity to observe friends and peers working hard and achieving success.

CHAPTER 8

Finding Confidence: Pillar Six

Bart is in third grade, and he's dreading the school holiday concert coming up in six weeks. It's a tradition for the third graders to play a series of holiday songs on the recorder while students in the other grades sing. Bart is overwhelmed by this idea because he doesn't believe in his ability to learn the recorder well enough to play in the concert. He doesn't want to "look stupid"; thus, he refuses to practice at home and does not fully participate in music class while the other students are learning and practicing.

Bart's sister Abby, also in third grade, has a completely different outlook on learning the recorder. While she also sees it as a challenge, she embraces the challenge and jumps fully into the learning and practicing. Playing the recorder comes quickly and naturally to her. Because of this, Abby feels confident in music class and is eager to show off her emerging ability to play the recorder. While she doesn't yet feel competent by any means, she's making progress, and that progress is reinforcing her commitment to stick with the process of learning.

We can see that the problem here isn't Bart's ability or inability to learn to play the recorder. The problem is that Bart's historically low confidence makes him reluctant to engage in activities that he perceives as challenging. Bart is an extremely bright and capable child, but he has limited belief in his own abilities. When learning anything new, there is a process. And it is the confidence to engage in this process and stick with it that builds feelings of competence and success over time. This confidence to try despite perceived challenge is vital.

Building Confidence in Children Who Are Struggling

Bart and Abby provide a perfect example of the fact that some children are naturally more confident than others. We don't always know why one child is confident while another is not. Yet, we can speculate on possible reasons:

- Children who are able to accomplish things more easily early in life may become more confident as a result.
- Positive social relationships that provide children with reinforcement early on may make them more confident.
- Positive experiences in general may lead to early confidence.
- Conversely, the lack of these positive variables may lead to a lack of confidence.

Children like Abby see a challenge and are naturally drawn in because they believe they can meet the challenge. Others, like Bart, are quicker to doubt themselves and their abilities. And we know that self-doubt makes it very difficult to feel confident. For elementary-school-age children, challenges can come in many forms, like learning to read, learning a new instrument, taking a test, organizing their schoolwork, giving a presentation, learning a new sport, performing well in a match or an important game, and even flying in an airplane for the first time. Confidence plays a central role in allowing kids to meet the challenge and perform up to their potential. Too many children miss the opportunity to reach their potential in different areas because they don't have the confidence to try.

The other potential pitfall of not participating in something because of low confidence is that low confidence can erode other areas of the child's life. When this happens, the child continues to miss out on many things and thus doesn't have the opportunity to recognize his true potential in any area. Providing the tools for kids to build confidence in all domains is one way to ensure that they have the chance to maximize their potential over time. A child's confidence and belief in her ability to succeed is a vital element of resilience.

What can be done to help a child like Bart, who lacks the confidence to play the recorder in the holiday concert? We can add a set of tools to his toolbox to help him believe in his ability to learn the recorder along with his classmates. Such tools might include building trust in his abilities through practice and positive reinforcement, creating positive self-talk strategies and learning breathing exercises to help him relax and better regulate his emotional responses. The good news is that these tools will also help him to meet other challenges, while increasing his overall sense of belief in himself. Children who believe in themselves and their ability to succeed despite challenge are generally more likely to try again when things don't go as planned, and to keep moving forward despite obstacles. And remember, these traits are key to reaching potential. Children who continue to sit on the sidelines because of low confidence miss out on many opportunities.

OVERCOMING CHALLENGES WITH CONFIDENCE

In school, confident students are often more resilient in that they tend to believe in their ability to succeed despite challenge, despite times of difficulty, and even when things go wrong. This is a particularly important skill to foster in elementary students as it sets a foundation for them to succeed later in school and beyond. Confident students – those who believe in themselves and can talk themselves through challenges – are more likely to maximize their potential in all areas of life in a self-reliant and self-assured way.

Confidence starts with a commitment to try and the courage to follow through on reaching goals and dreams despite resistance, challenges or setbacks. Parents, teachers, coaches, community leaders and many others play a central role in this process. We can offer tools to bolster confidence, and we can support children in their learning as a way of boosting confidence. It's important to note here that children don't always demonstrate the same level of confidence in all domains. For example, a child may be very confident in math but much less so in reading. Or a child may be very confident in social situations or in sports and much less confident in a classroom setting. Confidence can vary across domains in a vast number of ways. The key is to find the places where a child demonstrates confidence in herself and build on that, so that the idea that success is possible with effort and persistence touches all aspects of the child's life.

Tyler's Negative Belief System

Like Bart with the recorder, Tyler, who is eleven years old and in fifth grade, believes he "can't do it," whatever "it" is. He believes that "everyone is better than me at everything." It doesn't matter if Tyler is in the classroom trying to do something new, or even something he's done many times before, or if he is on the baseball field or soccer field. This negative belief system somehow has come to define Tyler's view of himself. It's not clear why Tyler feels this way, but this early belief system is affecting his self-esteem and his ability to live up to his potential in all areas of his life.

Tyler could use some coaching to help him identify his strengths and find ways to use them to his advantage. This will help him to develop an overall belief in his abilities. Additionally, providing Tyler with tools to manage his emotional response to challenging situations as they arise will help shift his outlook on what he is capable of. Once he understands what it feels like to be in a coherent, self-regulated emotional state and learns to integrate this state into his day-to-day way of being through practice and repetition, Tyler will have a much easier time accessing – and, more importantly, believing in – his true abilities.

My Story: Lack of Confidence Leads to Underperformance

We've seen that confidence is essential to moving forward despite challenge, and this in turn helps build resilience and maximize potential. Now I'd like to give an example from my own childhood of the opposite: how a lack of confidence in one area, if left unaddressed, can lead a child to underperform in that area.

I was in fifth grade when I had a significant medical setback that caused me to miss about three months of school. When I finally came back, I figured I would resume my life as normal. But it wasn't that easy. The first challenge was lack of social support: following my prolonged absence, many of my peers were unsure how to interact with me. The second challenge was academic: despite significant tutoring when I was out of school recovering, after I returned my teacher labeled me as needing extra help in math and put me into a new, lower, math group. I quickly internalized this label and began to believe that I wasn't as capable as before, and thus my confidence in math plummeted. This made me feel sad and frustrated. Up until this point, I had considered myself quite competent in math and hadn't been intimidated by anything that came my way in math class. But now I questioned my abilities, and my performance in math class reflected this lack of confidence and belief that I could perform as I once had. To be fair, it is possible that I needed the extra attention in math after my prolonged absence. Yet, I believe there were other ways to offer me the extra help without the definitive label.

While I never fully recovered my confidence in math, fortunately this didn't erode my confidence in other domains. In time, my social confidence returned and I essentially resumed life as it had been, except for math. I was able to compensate over time and build on my strengths in other academic areas, which allowed me to be a confident student through college and my doctoral program in psychology. Great support at home, along with support from a group of good friends and their families, is what allowed this to happen. Thus, I was able to internalize a sense of competence and my own ability to succeed despite challenge.

As I think back on the experience now, I realize how helpful specific tools would have been for coping with the expectations and negative labels thrown my way during this experience. Tools to help me stay engaged and positive when math started to get too difficult would have allowed me to make better sense of what was happening, and perhaps I wouldn't have lost so much confidence in my math abilities.

Sam and Peter: Confidence in Sports

Young athletes must believe in their skills and abilities in order to succeed in sports, whether they are just learning or are more experienced and already competing. Here are a couple of examples – Sam, a tennis player, and Peter, who does Kung Fu – to illustrate how important this is and how such confidence can be fostered.

Nine-year-old Sam, a fourth grader, is in his first year of tennis match play, a competitive weekend program for junior tennis players. He is excited about the chance to play every Sunday, but he struggles much of the time with his confidence. Although his skills are good enough to play and even win on some days, he doesn't believe that they are. Until he believes in his abilities, his play will suffer and the results of his matches will reflect his low confidence. Sam would benefit from tools to help him boost his confidence as a tennis player, such as working on coping skills, developing a practice plan, and working on managing distraction.

Peter, twelve years old and in sixth grade, feels very self-conscious when he does any physical activity. He lacks confidence and worries that other children will laugh at him because he doesn't know what he is doing. But his parents have been encouraging him to take a Kung Fu class, and after much resistance he has finally agreed.

Now Peter needs tools to start believing he can succeed in Kung Fu. One tool that helps is that Peter creates a vision of himself as successful, so he can think about what that would look like and what it would feel like. Peter also makes a plan for practicing skills and integrating them into his daily life. With this kind of practice, learning happens and the Kung Fu moves become easier and more natural for Peter. He begins to develop authentic confidence in his abilities on the Kung Fu mat.

In time, this confidence begins to transfer to other areas of his life (e.g., the classroom, social relationships, other sports). In bolstering his confidence, Kung Fu serves as a powerful catalyst for Peter to move forward towards his potential in many different areas. He becomes more engaged, and his progress is obvious. Peter is becoming more resilient and learning the importance of persistence and hard work.

Confidence Is a Catalyst for Moving Forward

One of the greatest gifts we can give children is tools and reinforcement to feel good about their ability to succeed through hard work and persistence. This will provide a strong foundation for resilience and the realization of potential over time. Fostering confidence in children and their abilities helps defend against bullying by those who are not able to fully appreciate the differences among us. The child with stable confidence will be able to walk away from a bully and stand up for what she believes in. Confidence also provides the foundation for learning: trying and mastering new skills. Confidence is a catalyst for moving forward that is at the core of a resilient child.

Pillar Six Action Steps: Finding Confidence

Here's a list of strategies that can help a child who is struggling with finding confidence in school or in sports. Parents and teachers can get started on some of these right away; others may require individually tailored coaching by a certified professional.

In the Classroom

- Encourage the child to embrace challenge and see it as an opportunity.
- Demonstrate that practice and competence build confidence.
- Help the child believe in her ability to succeed.
- Encourage the child to focus on positive self-talk.
- Help the child identify strengths and use them to compensate for challenges.
- Show the child how to develop a vision for success.
- Find places where the child demonstrates confidence in himself and build on that, so that all aspects of the child's life are touched by the idea that success is possible with effort and persistence.

In Sports

- Encourage the child to do the best he can, without expectations for outcome.
- Help the child develop a practice plan.

- Work with the child to create a vision for success – what would it look like and feel like?
- Teach the child coping skills to deal with mistakes and not lose focus or confidence.
- Work with the child to manage distraction.
- Find sports where the child demonstrates confidence in herself and build on that, so it spills over into other sports as well.

CHAPTER 9

Creating Optimism: Pillar Seven

Teddy is ten years old and has a very positive outlook on life. He's a happy boy and he always thinks about what is possible in each moment of each day. Teddy is full of plans and hope, and he's generally confident that things in his life will work out even when he's faced with a challenge. He is naturally optimistic. For example, when something goes wrong at school or he has a bad day overall, Teddy doesn't get bogged down with all that went wrong. He may acknowledge the negative occurrence, but he doesn't let it get to him for too long. He's able to move forward. In this way, Teddy's sense of optimism is a useful tool in helping him to navigate the various challenges that he will inevitably face in elementary school and beyond. It also makes him more resilient by helping him to move forward despite challenge.

Fritz is Teddy's best friend. Like Teddy, he's ten years old and in the fourth grade. But Fritz has a much different outlook on life than Teddy: he is much more bothered by the daily challenges he faces at school and in other areas of his life. For example, if Fritz feels like he did poorly on a test or an activity, he gets stuck thinking about what went wrong and going over and over the various ways that things could have or should have been different. And to take it a step further, Fritz has a difficult time believing that he will do better the next time. To borrow the old cliché, Fritz's glass tends to be half empty most of the time, while Teddy's glass is usually at least half full. Challenges are much more difficult for Fritz to navigate because of his tendency to see things in a negative context, and because it's difficult for him to embrace the idea of possibility and the idea that different outcomes are possible in the future.

Optimism: A Launchpad for Moving Forward

The examples of Teddy and Fritz show how an optimistic outlook can benefit children by helping them move through and beyond challenge. Helping children to maintain their sense of optimism over time and as they're exposed to the inevitable disappointments and realities of life is important to their overall well-being and resilience. We can help by arming children early in school and at home to develop coping skills and tools such as these:

- The ability to see what's positive in their world
- The ability to cultivate gratitude daily
- The ability to identify and use their strengths
- The ability to problem-solve when faced with challenge

These skills will enable them to manage setbacks while maintaining a generally positive outlook both in the present and into the future. In this way, optimism fosters resilience by making it easier for children to move forward despite challenge. It's important to help all children to develop these tools, whether they're naturally optimistic or not. Even a naturally optimistic child may need help maintaining that positivity in the face of the inevitable disappointments and challenges of childhood and beyond.

Some children, like Teddy, are naturally more optimistic than others. This fundamental outlook has the power to determine a lot in terms of the decisions children make and how they look at life's challenges, both positive and negative. If they expect things to go well, the chance that they will go well is that much greater. If, on the other hand, a child expects from the outset that something will not go well, chances are greater that it will not. The idea here is that seeing possibilities before seeing the obstacles is a positive attribute that helps children move forward despite challenges. It is important to note here that being optimistic does not negate the real-life challenges that we all encounter; it simply provides a framework for managing these challenges and moving forward with greater ease despite them.

My Story: How One Person Can Make a Big Difference

I faced a major challenge in fifth grade when my shunt failed and I needed numerous complex surgeries to fix the problem. Whenever something like this happened, it was always a scary and painful experience for me. Yet, I was fortunate to have a strong support team in my parents, family, friends, teachers and doctors. The people in my life helped me to get through the tough moments by offering support and sometimes distracting me from my medical reality. And luckily, my fundamental sense of optimism allowed me to focus on the possibility of moving forward while still acknowledging the reality of the challenge I faced.

During one prolonged hospital stay after a particularly difficult series of shunt revisions, a young resident, Dr. R, frequently came by to talk with me outside of the scope of her official duties. She was kind and supportive and took the time to engage me in discussions about the things that interested me, which at that time were becoming a doctor and playing tennis. The fact that these interactions remain fresh in my mind thirty-five years later is a testament to the impact they had on me. I am certain that by taking an active interest in me and in my recovery, Dr. R helped me to regain my underlying optimistic outlook, which had been buried by the medical challenges I experienced during those months. I know for certain that this was vital to my overall recovery and ability to get back to school and living my life.

Connor's Disappointments

Sometimes it's not as easy for children to maintain an optimistic attitude over time. When Connor was a little boy, he was always happy and optimistic. As time went on and he experienced some of the inevitable challenges and disappointments that life brings, his natural sense of optimism started to change and his baseline outlook became much more pessimistic. Now in the fourth grade, Connor is a good student but he tends to start most experiences and tasks believing that they won't work out. Sadly, he's become pessimistic about friendships and social issues at school because of a few pivotal experiences in which boys he thought were his friends became "mean" and acted like bullies. For Connor, who is a thoughtful, sensitive child, this change in his classmates' behavior is particularly upsetting and he can't let it go and move forward. Connor's pessimistic outlook is eroding his schoolwork and making him much less confident in his ability to succeed on assignments and tests. While he's a strong student, his fundamental lack of optimism is making him lose confidence and belief in his academic abilities. Even when things turn out better than anticipated, Connor has a hard time shifting out of his pessimistic mindset.

What kinds of tools can help build resilience in a child like Connor, who has so much going for him but lacks the ability to believe in himself? We can help him add a set of tools to his toolbox that will foster optimism about what is possible:

- Help him to identify the good things in his day
- Create a list of positive self-talk statements
- Help him to develop a list of the things he is good at
- Help him develop the courage to walk away from bullies

With these tools, Connor will be much better prepared to see the positive side of situations, and this will enable him to let go of the negative more easily and move forward. He will be better equipped to cope with his feelings of sadness and disappointment that come because of an interaction with a school bully who Connor thought was a friend.

Optimism in Sports: Team Dynamics

What happens on a team when some members are optimistic about an outcome and some are not?

The Rangers, a team of nine year olds, are in their first playoff game of the Little League post-season. They're playing the Padres – the best team in the league. Half of the Rangers' players are optimistic about their ability to win the game, and the other half are completely sure they will lose.

When you feel you are going to lose, it's difficult to maintain a sense of optimism that a more positive outcome is possible. When you believe you're going to win from the outset, it is much easier to maintain that sense of optimism.

The Rangers' coach understands how important it is for all the players to be optimistic, and he rallies the less optimistic team members to shift their perspective as the game starts. The coach's job gets easier as the Rangers get off to a strong start and score four runs in the first inning. At that point, the more pessimistic players begin to believe in the possibility of winning the game. As the game goes on, the Padres rally, and the score remains close until the end. Yet, with solid teamwork and support among the players, and encouragement from the coach through the ups and downs of the game, the entire team believes they can win the game. The Rangers' coach cultivates even more optimism in his players by encouraging the boys to focus on one play at a time and one thing that they can do during each play to add to the team's success.

By staying focused and in the moment, the team doesn't think about all the what-ifs or the outcome of the game; instead, the boys focus on each moment as it happens and do their individual best. The Rangers start to notice their small successes in the field and at the plate, building momentum. Who knows if this belief in the possibility of winning is what pushes them over the edge. Yet, the collective optimism of the team and the coach helps all the boys come together and play their best baseball to win that first playoff game.

How Optimism Fosters Resilience

These ideas about optimism tie together many of the concepts discussed earlier in the book and are linked to resilience and moving forward despite challenge. Optimism not only fosters resilience, but also the courage to try. Overall, children who are optimistic tend to demonstrate an eagerness to try new things, as they believe in the possibility of a positive outcome despite potential challenge. And when optimistic children do encounter an obstacle, they can get back up and keep moving forward despite it. Even more important, they aren't afraid to face the challenge in the first place.

Fostering optimism in children is very important. An optimistic outlook helps children focus on the good around them. It helps them to stand up for the underdog and to walk away from conflict. It helps them take positive steps forward because they understand that there are possibilities beyond what is happening in the moment. In this way, optimism makes children more resilient in managing the challenges that life brings. As we have seen through this chapter, some children are naturally more optimistic in their overall outlook while others will only be optimistic in specific areas of their lives. To reap the more global benefits of optimism in children, it will be important to provide them with the tools to develop a greater sense of optimism across the domains of their lives. Optimism will add to children's ability to cope and move forward despite challenge, ultimately making them more resilient.

Pillar Seven Action Steps: Creating Optimism

Here's a list of strategies that can help a child who is struggling with creating optimism in school or in sports. Parents and teachers can get started on some of these right away; others may require individually tailored coaching by a certified professional.

In the Classroom

- Help the child to see something positive in every situation before seeing the obstacles.
- Provide opportunities to cultivate gratitude, such as a daily gratitude journal.
- Show the child how to identify and use his strengths to his advantage.
- Help the child to focus on what is possible.
- Help the child learn to manage challenges without being overwhelmed.
- Encourage the child to use positive self-talk.
- Help the child to stay focused in the moment.
- Build belief in self and ability to succeed by providing positive feedback and constructive ideas for improvement.

In Sports

- Encourage the child to focus on the love of the game.
- Help the child to believe in herself and her ability to succeed by providing positive feedback and constructive ideas for improvement.

- Encourage the child to stay focused in the moment and not worry about the bigger picture.
- Help the child to move beyond challenges by continuing to play after missing a shot or playing badly.
- Encourage the child to use positive self-talk.
- Notice the child's small successes and point them out.
- Be an example and embrace fun!

CONCLUSION

What the Kids Have to Say

My intent in writing this book was to capture the real-life human experience of what it means to be resilient in childhood and beyond. In order to accomplish this goal, I shared aspects of my own early experiences with facing and overcoming challenges, and I shared composite stories of children today that also, in many ways, reflect aspects of my own experiences over time. Viewed through my lens as a psychologist, a performance coach and a mom of elementary-school-age children, these examples provide a solid foundation for evaluating when and why kids can use help building toolboxes of strategies to help them master the seven pillars of resilience outlined in this book.

To further flesh out these ideas, I interviewed six children to get their thoughts. These are not clients; they are simply kids I know (identified by pseudonyms). I was curious to see if they would understand what each pillar means and why it is important in their lives. Their responses are enlightening and add depth to the human element of what this book is all about. They bring the concept full circle by highlighting how children can make sense of and live these ideas. For some, it will come naturally. For others, less so. But one thing is certain: all kids benefit when the adults in their lives support them and recognize when they need a hand.

With that, I'll turn it over to them. Here's what the kids have to say.

The Kids
Anne, age 8
Cody, age 9
Eliana, age 9
Tyler, age 8
Emily, age 9
Will, age 9

TOLERATING FRUSTRATION AND MANAGING EMOTIONS: PILLAR ONE

What does this mean?

"It means to calm down." –Anne

"In tennis or golf, when I hit a bad shot it (just) means it is a bad shot, and (I should) think about the next shot." –Cody

"Calm down." –Eliana

"It means to not yell and to think about your actions." –Tyler

"It means to control yourself." –Emily

"If you don't, it is disruptive to classmates." –Will

Why is it important to manage emotions and tolerate frustration?

"It is important so you won't say things you will regret." –Anne

"Because if you get mad about a bad shot, you will just hit more bad shots and will get really mad." –Cody

"It helps to calm down so you don't lose a friend." –Eliana

"Because you get in trouble if you don't." –Tyler

"If you don't, you will fall apart - get bad grades, get in trouble, lose friends." –Emily

"Since you could get in big trouble, you need to keep calm and think about why you are upset." –Will

Navigating Friendships and Social Pressures: Pillar Two

What does this mean?

- "It means I try to be nice and do what I can to be the best person I can be." –Anne
- "If they put pressure on me, if they want me to do something I don't (want to do), I walk away." –Cody
- "It means telling my friends I can be what I want in a game, not what they want me to be." –Eliana
- "Ask them to stop and if that does not work, walk away." –Tyler
- "It means to manage arguments." –Emily
- "They could be trying to make you do something bad." –Will

Why is it important to navigate friendships and social pressures?

- "People won't bully and will be nice." –Anne
- "If your friends want you to do something bad, you could get in trouble. I want to stay safe." –Cody
- "It is important so I can be who I want to be." –Eliana
- "Otherwise you would have to do something you did not want to do." –Tyler
- "If you don't, you won't have any friends." –Emily
- "Not doing it could lead to bad choices." –Will

SUSTAINING FOCUS AND ATTENTION: PILLAR THREE

What does this mean?

"It means being in the zone. If you focus, you can achieve your goals." –Anne

"Pay attention to your work. Listen to your teacher and coach." –Cody

"Focus means paying attention." –Eliana

"Listen to the teacher. Do as you are told." –Tyler

"When you focus, you are not distracted." –Emily

"If you are not focusing, you won't know what to do. You need to know what to do." –Will

Why is it important to sustain focus and attention?

"It lets me ignore things I don't need." –Anne

"It will let you learn more and be better. It will help you remember." –Cody

"I need to focus to learn." –Eliana

"If you don't, you will get in trouble and have to do laps." –Tyler

"You can't finish what you are doing without focus." –Emily

"Not focusing leads to bad consequences, and no one wants that." –Will

Developing Courage: Pillar Four

What does this mean?

"Courageous people do cool things." –Anne

"You believe in yourself and what you can do. It gives you faith that your next shot will be better." –Cody

"Courage is when you are brave." –Eliana

"To be able to stand up to your friends or teammates if they do something mean." –Tyler

"Courage gives you a reason to do something. It lets you move forward." –Emily

"Courage lets you do more." –Will

Why is it important to develop courage?

"Courage lets you push away things that bother you." –Anne

"It will let you give 100% and you will do well." –Cody

"You need courage to do things even when you are nervous." –Eliana

"If you don't, you will get bullied." –Tyler

"Without courage, you don't have the need to move forward." –Emily

"If you have more courage you can do more. You are lonely and sad without courage." –Will

Building Motivation: Pillar Five

What does this mean?

"Motivation is moving forward in hard times." –Anne

"Motivation lets you keep going." –Cody

"Motivation lets you get things done. You need motivation to do things." –Eliana

"If you aren't (motivated), you won't get it right in sports and you won't be very good, and you won't do well in school." –Tyler

"Motivation gets you started. It moves you forward." –Emily

"Motivation helps you do things." –Will

Why is it important to build motivation?

"It is important so you can keep moving forward." –Anne

"It helps you believe in yourself." –Cody

"If you are motivated to do your homework, you will learn something new." –Eliana

"Because if you are not motivated, you won't do well in school or sports." –Tyler

"If you don't have motivation, you don't have a reason to do what you are doing." –Emily

"Motivation is important because without it, you might be sad and grumpy. It makes you more helpful." –Will

CONFIDENCE:
YEAR SIX

What does this mean?

"It means, 'I can do this.' But you can't be too confident. You need to be flexible too." –Anne

"Being able to think, 'I can do this.'" –Cody

"Confidence means, 'I can do this.'" –Eliana

"If you are not confident, then you probably won't do well and you will be bored. School is more fun if you are confident." –Tyler

"Confidence is sort of like courage. You are confident in yourself and courageous for others." –Emily

"Confidence is feeling you are going to do well." –Will

Why is it important to find confidence?

"Confidence lets you do things. But you need balance and flexibility, too." –Anne

"It lets you do stuff. It lets you do your best." –Cody

"Confidence is sort of like courage but not exactly the same. Confidence lets you try and it lets you do your best." –Eliana

"School is more fun if you are confident." –Tyler

"You need confidence so you don't get scared." –Emily

"Without confidence, you won't know what to do. With confidence, you will know what to do." –Will

CREATING OPTIMISM: PILLAR SEVEN

What does this mean?

"You have hope and are pretty sure. It is a feeling that things are going to go well." –Anne

"You believe you will be good in the future." –Cody

"Optimism means, 'I can work this out.'" –Eliana

"Keep your head in the game and don't feel bad for yourself or get frustrated." –Tyler

"Optimism is focus and courage mixed together." –Emily

"Optimism is being happy and doing your best." –Will

Why is it important to create optimism?

"Optimism is important for when a bad thing happens so you won't collapse." –Anne

"Because it is important to believe you are good and can help others." –Cody

"Optimism gives me more confidence and lets me believe in myself." –Eliana

"Nothing is fun if you don't have optimism." –Tyler

"If you don't have optimism, you fall apart." –Emily

"You will be grumpy without it. You need it to do well." –Will

RESOURCE LIST

Following are resources that inform my writing and my practice and may prove useful to the reader who wants to further explore the ideas outlined in this book.

Books:

Erikson, E. H. *Childhood and Society.* New York: Norton, 1950.

Erikson, E. H. *Childhood and Society* (2nd ed.). New York: Norton, 1963.

Erikson, E. H. *Identity: Youth and Crisis.* New York: Norton, 1968.

Websites:

HeartMath Institute website: www.HeartMath.org

Dr. Kate Lund's sports coaching website: www.pugetsoundsportspsychology.com

AUTHOR'S BIOGRAPHY

Dr. Kate Lund is a licensed clinical psychologist and performance coach with more than fifteen years of experience. She has specialized training in medical psychology from Shriners Hospital for Children in Boston, Massachusetts General Hospital, and Beth Israel Deaconess Medical Center, all of which are affiliated with Harvard Medical School, and she is an adjunct instructor in Psychology at Bastyr University in Seattle.

Dr. Lund uses a strengths-based approach in working with students, athletes and teams to improve their mental game in school, sports and life while helping them to reach their full potential. Additionally, she has a special interest in working with athletes recovering from injury, helping them cope and maintain their mental edge. Dr. Lund played collegiate tennis; these days, she is an avid golfer and fitness swimmer.

Dr. Lund writes and speaks on a variety of topics aimed at empowerment and the development of one's true potential. Her children's book *Putter and the Red Car,* published last year, is the first in a series she is writing for young children linking her lifelong passion for Airedale terriers with such ideas as adapting to change, building resilience and the power of possibility. Dr. Lund lives in Washington State with her husband, two boys and a lively West Highland White terrier named Squirt.

Dr. Lund offers individually tailored coaching programs in the following areas:

- Resilience Coaching
- Sports Psychology and Mental Game Coaching
- Positive Psychology Coaching
- Emotional Intelligence Assessment and Coaching

Made in the USA
Lexington, KY
24 June 2017